This Hill I Climb

(Complete 4-Volume Series)

*A Poetic Journey on the
Road to Redemption*

By
E.A. James

FM Publishing Company
Cherokee, NC 28719

This Hill I Climb (Complete 4-Volume Series)
A Poetic Journey on the Road to Redemption

Published by:

FM Publishing Company
P.O. Box 215
Cherokee, NC 28719
United States of America
www.fmpublishingcompany.com

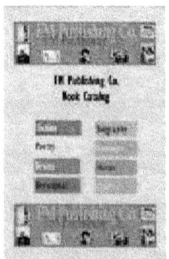

Unless otherwise indicated, all Scripture quotations are taken from The New King James Version. Copyright © 1982, Thomas Nelson, Inc. Publishers. Used by permission.

Copyright © 2010 by E.A. James. All rights reserved. No part of this publication may be reproduced, stored in a retrieval system, or transmitted by any means – electronic, mechanical, photographic (photocopy), recording, or otherwise – without written permission from the publisher.

Printed in the United States of America
ISBN 9781931671088
Library of Congress Control Number 2010935031

Poetic Contents

Part One – In the Valley 6
    Introduction 7
    Love Rocks 8
    Lost Rocks 9
    Stumbling Rocks 10
    A Fine Line 11
    Wild Rice 12
    Canceled Check 14
    Ode to the Entertainment Book 15
    Jail Bait 16
    Your Journey Notes & Reflections 19

Part Two – Climbing, Slipping, and Sliding 22
    Introduction 23
    A Sinner's Testimony 24
    Forgiven 26
    Thank You Father for Our Land 28
    Tears for Molly 30
    Nothing But the Truth 31
    One Family Tree 32
    The Child and the Cowboy 33
    Your Journey Notes & Reflections 36

Poetic Contents (cont'd)

Part Three – On the Mountaintop 39
   Introduction 40
   Life with Our Heavenly Father 41
   Holy Harmony 43
   My Neighbor, Myself 45
   Solo 47
   Alone, Never Lonely 49
   Acquired Taste 50
   The Feast of Yahweh (God) 51
   Casino Con 53
   Why Are You Marching? 57
   Your Journey Notes & Reflections 61

Part Four – Reaching Back 64
   Introduction 65
   Twenty Years Young 66
   In Memory of Tina 68
   In Memory of Jerry 70
   In Memory of Andrew 72
   When All Stood Still 73
   The Purpose of Marriage 74
   Forever Hold Your Peace 75
   O' The Beat of Obedient Hearts 78
   Sweet Silent Symphony 80
   Your Journal Notes & Reflections 81

Poetic Contents (cont'd)

Part Five – Redemption 84
    Introduction 85
    Redemption Time 86
    Roots Dye But Never Die 88
    By No Other Name 89
    Holding Out and Moving Ahead 90
    Recognizing the Counterfeit 91
    Taking the Good with the Bad 92
    Not Without My Armor 93
    The Right to Choose Life 94
    Finishing the Race 95
    Taking Out the Garbage 96
    My Turn is Coming 97
    I Feel Therefore I Am 98
    Fit As a Fiddle 99
    A Position of Dignity 100
    Death Be Not Proud 101
    Your Journal Notes & Reflections 102

About the Author 106

Publication and Catalog Ordering Information 107

Part One

In The Valley

Introduction

This Hill I Climb is one author's "poetic" 40-year journey on her road back to God and to Jesus Christ.

In the Valley is the first book of a four-part series. In these pages, the author opens up one of the dusty windows in the otherwise closed and secluded mansion of her unfinished life. As you peer through the window, your senses are awakened, prodded, pulled, and even pushed to the limits as you realize that at times the room resembles one in which you too may have lived.

All of us have, at one time or another, been "in the valley," or are even now "in the valley" in our walk as Yahweh's (God's) servants, that is, in our encounter with Jesus, the Master Fisherman. When we failed to acknowledge Him and did not love Him, He knowingly released the tension to give us more line. He allowed us to swim into deep muddy waters. Then, with the timing that only the Expert Fisher of Men can discern, His Holy Spirit begins to gently reel us in.

Once out of the water, we exercise our lungs. We gaze at our sinful reflections in the water. We see our true selves and discover that our feet have been planted on solid ground. And now the walk must begin.

It all starts in the valley. But it is the Holy Spirit that sweetly and gently entreats each of us to make that upward climb. And, as in all journeys, we learn that not only does it matter what steps we make and what paths we take, but we discover that our very choices make the eternal difference between Life and Death.

Love Rocks

She hurled her first rock.
It clanked against the spokes of Dan's new strawberry Schwinn.
She poised herself, ready to run.
Her bangs of wet pantyhose hid her eyes.
Flies tugged at watermelon stains on her pink cotton dress.
Dirt covered her crusty knees and white ankle socks.
Her black patent leather shoes, buried alive.
Dan's bike skidded in the dirt.
Her eyes darted to the deep tire tracks.
The ants now had a new freeway.
Dan spoke through a mouth full of marshmallows.
"Hey, wha's ya name?"
His shiny elephant tusks flashed in the sun.
Her fingers caressed another rock.
His head of cinnamon Cheerios exposed puppy-dog ears.
He was a chocolate Gumby in cut-off jeans.
She hurled the second rock. It thudded in the dirt.
Dan giggled for her to stop.
His bike tires made more dirt tracks.
She aimed at his back as he sped away.
At seven, the rocks had missed the mark.
Her target, Dan, was twelve, tall—taken.
By Connie, the dwarf with silver-studded earrings.
Her voice was a rusty hinge begging for oil.
"You betta leave Dan alone."
Smiling, she went hunting for bigger rocks.

Lost Rocks

She hurled the engagement ring at Wes' black leather jacket
The cheap rock bounced against his blood-shot Suzuki
Down into a muddy puddle, sinking from sight
At twenty-one, life was full of holes:
Her savings account and Wes' arms
Her ears and Wes' nose
Her small amber umbrella and Wes' condom in October
Her head sprouted half cooked fuzzy spaghetti braids
Tiny multi-colored meatballs smothered the spaghetti
She gave Wes tight jeans
He gave her loose teeth
His teeth and fingernails, the color of urine
His black wire hair, a grease fire in the making
He was a drunken bat with no wings
He could never separate the rain from her tears
The rain cried every day that December
Wes' bike growled, disappearing down Broadway
The dogs howled
The streets screamed in agony
She dripped back to the apartment
Her ears waited
The dogs finally slept
The rain still whimpered
Palm trees, corn bread, and beer slapped her face
Her black boots kicked through the puddles
She kicked against the prick of a big rock
It was hard, but not hers
Found lots of little rocks
Her socks began to drown
Wes' rock had rained away

Stumbling Rocks

She hurled and she hurled.
Woman against toilet bowl.
Head to head.
Her gums itched.
Her tongue had cleaned the floor.
She could only find eight toes.
The toilet had flushed her again,
Too many Vodkas on the rocks
Not enough rocks.
Thirty-five years, all alcoholic blurs.
Divorced, gray, out of toothpaste.
Another New Year's Eve.
Picture calendar of Alex
A crew cut pagan St. Bernard.
And Myra, a gold fingered yellow haired swine.
Out with the old, in with the new.
Their wine colored outfits with matching Mercedes.
The porcelain letter opener called her name.
Christmas gift from Mother.
Cute – Mother never writes.
Her head dragged along the sea-weed carpet.
Her nostrils drank in pine needles, stale eggnog, and bourbon.
The opener claimed Alex's dirt colored pupils.
Reciting resolutions would bring sobering sleep.
Stop smoking so much.
Give up dark chocolate.
Lose some weight next month.
Roast Alex's chest nuts.
Carve swine instead of turkey.
Send Mother a new telephone.
Change phone number.
Ask how she got into the Santa suit.
Most definitely, add more rocks.

A Fine Line

I hated you more than words
  Could possibly describe
Even though your DNA
  My blood transcribes

Never had a chance to know you
  Though your picture bears my face
You were never there to protect me
  To guard me from this place

One day I saw you paralyzed
  Stretched out within your tomb
How dare you leave me then
  A few years beyond the womb?

But how can one hate a shadow
  Whom time remembers no more?
There would be others to come
  And time to settle the score

At first I despised your image
  As it took on many a form
But it's hard to deny natural affection
  Created since one was born?

Your daughter's love for her father
  Transcended the walls of hate
She found her hapless healing
  In the arms of many a mate.

Wild Rice

Like Martin, I had a dream
Innocence—a distant memory
Rape—like yesterday
And the nightmare began

That special day of lucky rice
Something borrowed, something blue
Complete with bouncing baby
But the nightmare got better

My wedding bed—soiled with his drugs
Say hello to Poverty
Say hello to Pain
And where's my white picket fence?

Roaches and red beans and rice
Time to break away
Courts and red tape
No child support from turnips

And no lucky rice, but another said
"I'll take care of you"
His claws—much like the other
And the nightmare goes on

Did he slay my children's dreams?
Innocence—stripped and abandoned
Courts—he laughs in my dreams
Did you hear me screaming?

Jesus is there—He never left my side
I come home to God
My children—home to me
But where's that darn picket fence?

There it is—over there
See the burning cross of beams in your eye
Discrimination and Racism
Oh, and have a nice day

Soon, another hovers around me
I dream of a white Rice Day
But no "bended" knee, no ring, no kiss
And I still love him

This can't be a nightmare—I'm still awake
Bacon and eggs burn lovingly
My maternal mind remembers . . .
It's Mother's Day

Here they come—oh, those hugs!
No ring, no gown, no lucky rice
And still no white picket fence

But a heart out of tune
Beats nonetheless
And takes time to regain
    its melody.

Canceled Check

We've laughed and talked
We've quarreled and played
We've worked and planned
We've cried and prayed

We survived the heat, the cold
And staples and paper clips
We shoved paper back and forth
And taken bathroom trips

We've pretended for eight hours
As we worked our lives away
And smiled at our supervisors
Who devote no thought to pay

We soon learn it takes more
Than just eye pleasing the boss
And a job that another soon will fill
Has suddenly become our loss

So, here's to the Analyticals
Who forever will be right
To the popular Expressives
With no time to fight

To the hardworking Amiables
Who always take time to play
And to the frustrated Drivers
Who wanted it yesterday

So, this is how you say good-bye
And still save pride and face
For if the truth be fully known
You were glad to leave that place

Ode to the Entertainment Book

My heart skipped beating, my eyes were pleading
Oh, how my emotions shook
How could I neglect so great a task
And not procure an Entertainment Book?

I'd seen it perched there on its stand
It's cover, so glossy, so white
It's name in letters of liquid gold
That glistened in deep respite

The pages whispered, "Exquisite dining
For travel near and far
Come to fine hotels and ski resorts
In an elegant rental car"

Had I bought two, one could have served
As a year-long grateful gift
And I-I would have been satisfied
The epitome of college thrift

It cost but a few Sir George's bills
Totaling up to thirty and five
I'd have saved two thousand bucks
My budget would thus survive

0' Book, 0' Book, alas I cry
Are you gone forever more?
The word has come: no books remain
Good-bye Entertainment '94

Jail Bait

If patience is a virtue
She is the most virtuous of women
Solomon said "she does him good and not evil"
But she never married
And proverbs were written by men.

She knew he wouldn't remember
She would never forget
They say "love covers a multitude of sins"
Her prison guard cap covered his.

She could still feel his crusty charcoal claws
Silencing a testimony no one wanted hear
She could smell his steamy tobacco-breath
Smothering her with his foul fantasies.

He had the same cocky big-toothed grin
Her bowels begged to make him excrement
The cell door slammed shut
She could still hear the deafening click
Of his phallic pocket knife
Her forehead ached from the bloody "T"
He so skillfully sliced that day
Her missing maidenhood ached in remorse
Her limbs hated both of his tools.

She was Toni with an "I"
He was Tony with a "y"
She died that dreadful day
They gave him everlasting life
They had nothing in common.

She found no answers on the counselor's couch
She opted for the warden's instead
Seven years of prison politics
The warden wanted her
More than she wanted Tony.

Time was her only friend and she waited
Finally they brought Tony in
His cocky grin gave way to gravity
The promise of life was being reneged
His cell-mate murdered mysteriously
A "T" carved on the man's forehead
Three waiting and willing witnesses
The sentence was death.
The day she'd been dreaming of had come
She was dressed to kill
Her newly cleaned cap still covered
The blood-stained cross on her head
Her black belt buckled together
Her uniform united with lies
Her shiny black boots preciously prepared
With the mighty gospel of spit
She was the fisher of men.

No call from his gubernatorial savior
He was one of my chosen few
His lips pleaded for mercy
"Please, don't do this!"
"I'm innocent!"
"I don't want to die!"
She leaned into his sob-stained face
His stale breath mixed with fear
She admired the terror in his eyes
Mirroring her own seven years before

She too had pleaded for mercy
She too was innocent and didn't want to die
Her flesh had ripped
Face and heart scarred beyond repair
Every crevice of consciousness
Pierced by his manhood.

She hated the repentance now in his eyes
"Bless you my son," said the chaplain
"Thy sins be forgiven thee."
They definitely had nothing in common.

The chamber door closed his tomb
Tony's spirit now securely strapped
She waited for the signal
She gratefully grabbed the lever
His manhood now in her mighty hands

She gave herself to him completely
All her electrifying energy pulsated through him
His flesh ripped
His face scarred
She watched him writhe in eternal ecstasy
There he lay
His manhood spent.

Your Journey Notes & Reflections

Part Two

Climbing, Slipping, and Sliding

Introduction

<u>This Hill I Climb</u> is one author's "poetic" 40-year journey on her road to Jesus.

<u>Climbing, Slipping and Sliding</u> is the second book of a four-part series. In these pages, the author continues to take us on the journey with her. There is repentance, forgiveness, tears and joys. No matter what we encounter, no matter how hard the journey, our comfort is that our Father and Savior are always at our side. For He said He'd never leave us or forsake us.

We're growing and learning on the journey. We're learning who we are and how we fit into God's plans. We even gain glimpses of understanding as to why we're on this journey. More importantly, the Word of God is the light unto our path and the lamp unto our feet that illuminates our way. The terrain is rough and rocky, but we hang onto The Rock who is able to keep our feet from sliding.

So come let us climb. Let us press onward. The prize awaits us. Our Father and Savior (Messiah) has promised: He who has begun a good work in us will take us to the very end.

A Sinner's Testimony

I'm the one who's angry
My bowels blocked with hate
Resentment, jealousy and envy
Oh how they pack my plate

I'm reckless and immoral
Mistaking wrong for right
I serve a master called Self
No faith-I walk by sight

I heard a man proclaim
That he's the Son of God
My endeavor was to sever
This blasphemous facade

I sentenced him to die
And set a murderer free
I cried "Crucify him-
Let him cease to be!"

I'm the one who scarred him
With a bitter crown of thorns
My roar pricked him royally
Devouring moans and mourns

I'm the one who beat him—
His flesh was torn and sore
I'm the one who spat his name
And mocked the robe he wore

It was I who betrayed him
I also pierced his side
My kiss stung upon his cheek
And denied, denied, denied

Into his hands, into his feet
It was I who drove the stakes
I despised his forgiving eyes
Still pleading for our sakes

I'm the one who saw him dim
With a heartfelt painful sigh
As I heard him utter,
"*Yahweh (God), Yahweh (God), Lamasabachthani*"

I'm the one who disbelieved
When they said he rose again
Not to repent was my lament
"He won't forgive my sin"

Then one day I did believe
Yet still would disobey
Commit myself completely?
Tomorrow-not today

Now you know the way I am
Or rather, the way I was
I must confess I am the one
I'm the one
HE LOVES!

Forgiven

She moaned and moaned unto God
Her voice was heard in His ears
Her spirit cried out in desperation
Her joy so far away in years

Her sin filled her soul to the brim
The pain ran over the sides
She tried to gather the remains
But all rolled away like tides

Her lifeless hands wanted to leave
Disappear from life's angry stare
Her arms no longer to hold a loved one
The absence of warmth everywhere

Jesus would be there to hear her cry
He said He'd never leave her alone
He said to cast her cares upon Him
He'd take away her heart of stone

She wanted Him to chip the pieces away
That encompassed her soul that day
He held out his loving arms
His words He would never betray

She felt like she was fading away
Like she would cease to exist
How could she keep trudging along?
How could her faith persist?

Trust God with all her heart, she thought
Completely resign her soul
He will heal her heart from pain
And He would make her whole

Oh, the sin that no one knows
Just she and Jesus, alone
As yet to resist unto blood
Until the temptation is gone

"Father," she cries, "I need you now
My heart cries for relief
Doctors can only practice medicine
In healing, you alone are chief

"Take away this sickness deep inside
Make me worthy of your grace
I know I can never earn salvation
Only help me to run this race

"Into your hands I commit myself
My life to use as you will
Just mold me and I'll shine like gold
And sparkle on Zion's hill

Thank You Father for Our Land

Thank you Father for our land
It is only by your outstretched hand
It was you that brought me here
When do we celebrate the Sabbath year?

Hear the preacher speak the word
It's the best thing you've ever heard
He's the shepherd of the flock
But know that Jesus is our rock

Teaching is foremost and always first
You'll definitely learn to never thirst
Bring your troubles and lay them down
Keep on fighting 'till you earn your crown

If you listen, the Mothers will give you advice
Then you can whip the devil, not once, but twice
Keep on pushing and don't you balk
Honey, I'm a witness, it's a cakewalk"

Listen to the choir's ministry song
Come and join us and sing along
Lift your voices up on high
Praise His name-- don't be shy

Ask for prayer or give a praise report
On His blessings, God is never short
Then testify and jump and shout
Just know what you're shouting about

You can get baptized in Jesus's name
Just you bet you'll never be the same
Then you'll get filled with the Holy Ghost
Shouting Halleluyah from coast-to-coast

Ysrayl has a lot of work to do
Souls to save and some to renew
Jesus, our Rock – on him we'll stand
And He will lead us to the Promised Land

Tears for Molly

Don't look at me
I can't stand it when people stare
Pity is worse than death
It wears the mask of sympathy
Sometimes I want to shout, "go away,"
But my lips simply won't listen

I really should have hugged her—
But I didn't—I couldn't
Her cheeks formed an eternal kiss
And sickness gave her an awful haircut
She used to be so pretty
I wanted to be just like her
Of course, my doll, Molly,
Wanted to be just like me
I remember my long, cotton dress—
With violets that skipped whenever I did
They hid my tree-scarred knobby knees

I never dreamed of a white Christmas
I never dreamed of a black Christmas
I got both when I was born:
A drug letter from mama, "umbilically yours"
Mama smelled of honey and butter on my toast
That I always managed to get in my hair
She told me she loved me
My arms squeezed her with dittos of love

I learned in one day that my days would shorten
I had no time for green eggs and ham
I'd never have them in a tree
I'd never have them with a bee
The Cat in the Hat would never come back
And finding Spot was Dick and Jane's problem—It wasn't mine

Mama's veins are resting now—
Soon mine will too
"Now I know my H I V—tell me what you think . . . of . . . me?"

Nothing but The Truth

Matthew tell us the story
The one you told the Jews
Who rebelled and would not listen
When you tried to share the news
That Jesus is the true Messiah
Son of Yahweh (God) and King of Kings
Even one other King named Martin
Knew through Jesus freedom rings

Mark was the first to testify
To the Ysraylites who lived in Rome
Of Jesus, a servant on the move
Traveling miles from home
Healing the sick and feeding the poor
Accepting all who would come
He taught and worked many miracles
So that countless souls were won

Luke gave us an accurate account
Of the salvation that Jesus gives
Born of a virgin and the Holy Spirit
The perfect man, our Savior lives
Baptized by "one crying in the wilderness"
Unworthy to unlatch His shoes
"He must increase while I decrease
As a dove signified God's muse

Yochanan said in the beginning was the word
The same was with God and was God"
Jesus, Holy Master of all creation
Preached repentance wherever he trod
He said, "I am the Light of the world"
The Life, the Way, the Truth, the Gate
Cease from sin and keep my commandments
Watch, be ready, take heed, and wait!

One Family Tree

My family - *mi familia*
One who is familiar with me
One who knows my roots
One whose image I reflect
One bloodline
One name
That branches and sprouts
That connects and spreads
So that all Heaven and Earth take notice.

My family is in me
I am in my family
One body, many members
Who battle themselves
Sowing divisions
Sowing hate
Sowing pride
The thread of unity unravels
The soil slowly sifts away
The roots give way in agony.

One tree falls in the forest
One who hears it, is the
One who listens.

The Child and The Cowboy
(A Little Child Shall Lead Them)

After the cowboy turned down the preacher
  and said, "Go to church? No way!"
He went back to doing his chores
  and didn't finish until late in the day

A young child at the age of seven
  Had been listening as he sat by the road
He knocked on the cowboy's door
  with a quilt his mama had sewed

"Why, thank you," grinned the cowboy,
  "Thank you, child, very much
I always liked your mama's quilts,
  They have that personal touch

And how is she anyway," said the cowboy,
  "I ain't seen her up and around"
"Why, ain't you heard?" said the child
  "Last week they put her in the ground"

The cowboy couldn't say a word
  He hadn't known she was so ill
He'd been busy tending to his farm
  And making sure tomorrow's meal

The child wanted to talk about the preacher
  And how he'd been listening by
"When I heard you say no to the preacher
  Sir, all I could do was cry

You said there's folk at church
  Who say one thing and do another
I know at least one was true to God
  And that *one* was my mother

You said they sin six days a week
 And go to church on the seventh one
Well, mama prayed all week long
 And by then she still wasn't done

She read her Bible and studied her word
 'Til it was down off in her heart
It said not to forsake assembling together
 And sir, here comes the best part

She said when you truly want to know God
 And be truly washed of your sins
His Spirit draws you to His house, and
 Sir, why you just want to come in

And when they sing and praise and lift God's name
 Sir, now that's a joy to behold
You see in church I learned about Jesus—
 The greatest story ever told

I learned how he loved his Father's house
 And was obedient unto death
And how he forgave those who killed him
 Even with his dying breath

And how he rose on the third day
 Just so we can have eternal life
But I don't mean to bother you with scripture
 'Cause I know it cuts like a knife

I noticed you built on some more barns
 To house another cow or a foal
You're like that rich man, Yahweh (God) told him
 'Tonight I require your soul'

And I heard you tell that preacher
 You worship God in all you do
But by to the word my mama taught me
 I can see that just ain't true

And I say, yes, it's a miracle,
 Just watching a baby calf nurse
But I tell you if you don't accept Jesus,
 All your good is a curse

It's not just being morally good—
 Heck, I know, and I'm just seven
The devil got everybody believing
 That when we die we all go to heaven

I know I'm a child, but I have a request sir,
 Please consider your very last breath
'Cause there is a way that seems right to a man
 But the end thereof . . . is death."

Your Journey Notes & Reflections

Part Three

On The Mountaintop

Introduction

<u>This Hill I Climb</u> is the author's "poetic" 40-year journey on her road back to Yahweh (God) and to Jesus Messiah.

<u>On The Mountaintop</u> is the third book of a four-part series. Finally, after the long arduous journey with the author, we've reached the mountaintop. There is tranquility; there is peace. We revel in God's grace and His love. Our faith has been tested and we've passed some of the tests. We've failed others. But there we stand - on the mountaintop. God's presence is all around us. We bask in His Shekanah Glory.

We finally understand what Dr. King meant when he said, "I've been to the mountaintop, and I've looked over." We understand his serenity. We understand our Father and Savior's peace with His Father's will that He must, for all mankind, taste the cup of death. He'd been to the mountaintop. We understand the great light that shone in the eyes of God's humble and meek servant who led the children of Israel out of slavery. And, we truly understand the same light that knocked rebellious Saul from his high horse, to create Paul, an illuminating light for the Gentile nations to lead them to the mountaintop of God's grace and deliverance.

Here we stand. Our feet firmly planted. Our hearts and minds rooted and grounded in our Father's amazing truth. However, it has taken us to make it this far in the journey to realize that our perfecting has only just begun.

Life with Our Heavenly Father

Now to our earthly fathers we're told to give honor and praise
For in this we have God's promise that we will see many days
And just as our earthly fathers, through love, discipline and correct
Our Heavenly Father even more so, chastens; His goal: to perfect
The accuser and enemy tries to destroy God's name;
He lies and deceives and says God is to blame
He led man astray so that sin could abound;
But God foiled his plan and cursed him and the ground

Without our Heavenly Father there can be no life
For by Him we move and we breathe
So when our former darkness is dispelled in His light;
Newness of life we receive
Now we may not sing like angels and we may not preach like Paul
But all we have belongs to Him
So to Our Heavenly Father why not give all?

Jesus said, Our Father who art in Heaven, hallowed be thy name
And once you accept His precious Son
How can your life ever be the same?

Father, Son, and Holy Ghost; these three agree as one
So when Our Heavenly Father commands and speaks
Halleluyah, His will is done!

Now Like Abraham, God will call you out;
Saying "Be ye holy and separate, and never doubt"

Like Moses, He'll lead you to a mountaintop,
And you'll know what thou shalt do, *and* what thou shalt not

Like Yeshayah (Isaiah), He'll touch your lips with fiery coals;
And you'll shout "Send me, Father, *I'll* go to lost souls"

Like Yirmyah (Jeremiah), He'll send you to a rebellious nation,
Who will neither heed nor listen though they need salvation

Like Yehez'qel (Ezekiel), He'll say "Preach, so these dry bones can live;
Tell them, repent and their sins I'll forgive"

Like Daniel, He'll save you from a lion's den,
And bless you with wisdom to interpret dreams of men

Like Esther, He'll promote you to a higher place,
And humble you greatly for the task you must face

Like Ruth, He'll use your virtue to continue His plan,
For through her lineage came the Son of Man

Like Dawid, He'll renew a right spirit and clean up your heart,
And restore the joy of salvation that sin caused to depart

Like Jesus, you'll face betrayal, abuse and lies,
But He says "Endure the suffering, and you'll receive the prize"

Like the Disciples, He'll teach you how to walk, talk, and pray;
Like Peter, He'll teach you what it's best *not* to say

Like Paul (Sha'ul), He'll blind you and knock you off your high horse,
Then call you to preach the gospel with *His* anointed force

Like the bleeding woman whose faith made her whole,
He'll say "Cry out without shame, and I'll heal your soul"

And Like Yochanan (John), He'll reveal to you all things to come
And give you loving assurance that the victory is won

And to all his people who desire His mercy, His blessings, and heartfelt touch
He says, "Seek me, obey my word, be faithful with little, I'll bless you with much

So to you Our Heavenly Father, we praise your Holy Name
You alone are worthy, for you made your kingdom our aim

HOLY, HOLY, HOLY is Almighty Yahweh (God), His angels proclaim
By His grace, Life with Our Heavenly Father, we covet to obtain

Holy Harmony

They are the Holy Keys
  Played to show the way
Law reveals the weakness
  Grace then saves the day

As the keys blend together
  The black with the white
One played without the other
  Is like day without its night

For as keys have enharmonic
  Two notes—still one pitch
Law and Grace share a goal
  To lift the spiritual ditch

Treble sends a delicate melody
  Albeit, a tune called Grace
So pleasing it is to hear
  That He has pled our case

Bass then is the means
  By which all harmonize
Just as Law is God's agreement
  A standard to make us wise

Some say the Law was put to rest
  So that Grace could then abound
We even "hear" one note at rest
  While the other bursts with sound

But our Father is just and fair
  And allows all equal time
Perhaps the Law has been put to sleep
  And awaits its turn to shine

For out of Grace is born a love
  That no one dare deny
Producing loving obedience
  To words that cannot die

A dual glissando—indeed
  That depicts Law and Grace
Forever pitted in opposition
  A stand-off face-to-face

Who will win this gospel challenge
  As they charge so desperately?
Down the scales, is there collision?
  No, they land on middle "C"

For at the Cross is a Mediator
  Even so, a loving savior
With sacrificial outstretched arms
  To welcome both with favor

"The enemy is defeated!"
  Proclaims the powerful orator
"For I AM THAT I AM
  The one and only Creator!

"Law is fulfilled and Grace abounds
  Play this symphony to every nation
"Oh, take heed, all ye lands
  Herein lies *true* salvation!"

My Neighbor, Myself

*L*ast night I had a dream
could have sworn I was awake
but God said wake up
your neighbor's life's at stake

*O*ff I ran with all my might
had to go back for my clothes
I put on my best pair of shoes
the sandals—with no toes

*V*aliantly I took off again
ready to fight, ready to labor
when suddenly I wondered
Now just who is my neighbor?

*E*ach and every human being
said God with a heavy sigh
those who mourn in Zion
and those whose eyes are dry

*T*reat each one with love
though they may differ from you
understand who they really are
then you'll realize what to do

*H*elp them be the best they can be
and be slow to categorize
but teach and instruct them in my ways
and be careful of compromise

*Y*ou must live righteous before them
so as not to cause them to stumble
for you err not only when you sin
but when you complain and mumble

*N*ow I knew who my neighbor was
and I knew just what to say
I knew I had to live right before them
not just any kind of way

*E*ach beatitude came to mind
that Jesus spoke and taught
I must be humble in my spirit
if the Kingdom of Heaven is sought

I prayed to be meek and lowly
as Yahweh (God) said I should
I prayed to show kindness and mercy
and for actions that were good

*G*ive me a heart that is pure
to live peaceably with all men
let me think on the things of others
and their cause let me defend

*H*e said let it be as you have prayed
but be faithful in all you do
it is a sin to commit to your neighbor
and then not follow through

*B*y now I felt I was ready
Ready to cross that bridge
but halfway over my foot got stuck
my sandal was caught in the ridge

*O*h God, I cried, what do I do?
my neighbor needs my aide
but before I finished my prayer
a gentle hand in mine was laid

*R*eleasing my sandal from its snare
was my neighbor from the other side
thankful tears streamed down my face
and gone was my life-long pride

Solo

This is to the single mothers
Whose song we seldom sing
Those whose life is doubly hard
Yet dares to dance with dreams

Though life is a challenge for us all
The married have their mate
Silently the single mother sighs
As God says she must wait

Like the scriptural virtuous woman
She is diligent and she is wise
Yet she knows with just one voice
It's hard to harmonize

She remembers in times of old
As soprano in their duet
So much for roaming Romeo
When she once played Juliet

Watch her walk the high wire
As she balances her day
With kids and work and chores
And stress that makes her gray

At times she prays herself to sleep
The sorrow that nobody knows
But morning brings renewed hope
And faith to forget her woes

Still, she feels life's unfair
It's not how it's meant to be
A home needs mother and a father
For a child to be happy and free

Her children can be "cool" and cruel
And she'll suffer a fiery dart
But she sees the enemy for who he is
Mother's love heals her heart

For her child will say "I'm sorry"
To the arms which never closed
Yet tough love will allow them to reap
The sorrows they have sowed

She's a mother to be admired
For her courage and forthright strength
She will gladly give all she has
While others begrudge one-tenth

"It must be hard for you," they say
And she takes it all in stride
For God has truly seen her through
Yahweh (God) does provide

So we salute you single mothers
Your lives are our epiphany
For we know God through seeing you
And our souls sing a symphony!

Alone, Never Lonely

Another Valentine's Day and we're alone
no earthly mate to make our date
If you haven't anyone by January
They say it's already too late

Yet there is a peace we feel inside
the quiet joy of solitude
to meditate on Valentines past
who was pleasant and who was rude

Time to reflect on who we are
what makes us laugh and makes us cry
what can we bring to a relationship
to nurture it well or else watch it die

Husbands, wives, lovers, and others
Family, friends, and dates
Flowers, chocolates, and kisses
Our likes, loves, and hates

We don't want just any Valentine
but someone who loves our soul
that person who knows forgetting this day
could really cause heads to roll

Next year we may or may not be alone
but one thing you can bet for sure
We'll know who we are and what we need
Our decisions will be more mature

Acquired Taste

our bible is the Word of God
like gargling with garlic
"Thou shalt not . . . "
Aunt Mae's armpits and brother's jock strap
Johnny the pedophile's innocent smile

we tried to ignore the garlic
it became an ointment of onion
"Messiah died for you . . ."
called the "N-word" and "a credit to your race"
never called at all

we peeled the onion
and found a lesson of lemons inside
"All have sinned . . ."
a homeless child and a childless home
assault and battery across Betty's face

we kept the lemon seeds
they transformed into an orchard of oranges
"Be baptized in the name of Jesus for the remission of your sins . . ."
grandma's white bed sheets dancing in the sun
breath—after a dance with death

we planted the orange seeds
a tree sprang up with chocolate almond kisses
"Thou shalt love God with all your heart . . . love your neighbor as yourself . . ."
doing '80 on I-10 at 3 AM
passing gas and no one cares
understanding *why* we eat so much garlic.

The Feast of Yahweh (God)

The invitations have gone out
Now it's time to RSVP
For soon the bridegroom will arrive
For all the world to see

He seeks a glorious bride
Without wrinkle, spot, or blemish
Will he find what he seeks
When he declares "It is finished?"

Come, while the door is still open
For you he's reserved a place
Will you accept Yahweh (God)'s invitation
To come boldly to the throne of grace?

The ushers are there to greet you
With warmth and a loving smile
For they understand the choice you make
In your shoes they've walked that mile

So, enter into his gates with thanksgiving
Oh, come into his courts with praise
This is a time of righteous rejoicing
Filled with *"halleluyahs"* and "hoorays!"

If you thirst, come willingly to the waters
Proclaims the prophet: come eat, come buy
Why do you still spend and lustfully labor
For the things that cannot satisfy?

O' taste and see that Yahweh (God) is good
The meat of his word he'll delectably carve
But it's up to you to partake of this feast
Lest your inner man surely starve

Allow God's Spirit to move in your life
Convict, purge, and heal every wound
Feel free to shout and praise him
That is, if you can find room

For the same ushers with the humble smile
Who greeted you so meekly at the door
Are now going forth in a holy dance
And appear to have taken over the floor

After all, the feast is available to all
It's not every day the latter rain pours
And believe me the ushers *will* get theirs
So I advise you—come and get yours

So, let's usher in God's kingdom
Let's usher in His will, His way
Oh, usher in the joy of Yahweh (God)
And let him have control this day!

Casino Con

I remember my really first big win
Little did I know I'd be back again and again
And I was the one who would squeeze a dollar
So hard that even old George would holler

At first Laughlin's turnaround was all I would do
Twenty dollars to play with and then I was done
Quarters were too much for me to play
Nickels were surely the best name of the day

Exciting watching reels roll round and round
Bells ringing and dinging, my, what a sound
I found myself lost with no time and space
Of course no windows and clocks in that place

So much fun "quarters" were now my friend
This was the start of the graduated trend
Five times the money for five chances to win
Three Magic Mountains in a row it would send

I didn't even mind the Fort's 11 mile-drive
I was drawn to that place like a bee to a hive
Losing, disappointments, downright despair
But I took it in stride with my usual flair

Better luck next time with money to burn
On my way to a lesson too hard for me to learn
Debts, bankruptcy, and almost losing my house
Left looking and feeling like an unlucky louse

All right now I'm back on the right track
God is my supplier—with Him there's no lack
But Casino Arizona is right down the street
Play Wheel of Fortune for an exciting new treat

Some took a million dead presidents home
And the Casino itself built a brand new dome
You get a tax right off on the money you lose
Never mind you walk away without any shoes

And don't keep your vouchers for far too long
After 90 days, the cash date is gone
Found this out the hard way and no one cared
However, this information I freely shared

"People don't keep the vouchers that long
"90 Days Same as Cash?" Not in this case
But the casinos post the signs required by law
Albeit in the obscurest places that I ever saw

I noticed one man feverishly rubbing his head
He lost everything and had no money for bread
"I can't believe it," he said with a frown
"I was up so far, and then I went down."

Of course I don't do what the Heathen do
But the con cares nothing for Greek or Hebrew
Hey, I'm a child of God who is truly blessed
Deception warmly welcomed its willing guest

Now time to drink from the mighty Gila River
With even more slots that make spines shiver
Black Jack, Poker, Bingo and more
More chances means more chances to score

Five years gone by and no millions been won
It doesn't matter, the con has been run
Hundreds of thousands can be your regime
By simply investing in a mere penny machine

I can be rich beyond my wildest dreams
Can this really be as good as it seems?
Even Harrah's has added more Pennies inside
A lucrative business far, near, and wide

The games are fun with bonuses galore
Win three times, up to ten times and more!
Play 9 to 20 lines and maximize your credits
Never mind you'll also maximize your debits

Out of money? To the ATM you dash
Hurry to feed the slot every bit of your cash
For some reason we think we'll win every time
So, back to the ATM, again we're in line

If The Price is Right, to the showcase you go
Play Cliffhanger for a chance for more dough
Let Austin Powers get "shaggedelic" with you
His underground layer is reserved for a few

The Munsters, The Addams or Leopard's Spots
Grandpa's wild, Fester's fried—look—jackpots!
Drive the Road Rally or sail on Cleo's Nile
Or with 3 takeout orders, Mr. Lucky will dial

Jeanie will call you "Master" and dance and sing
Play with Wild Bears or the Elephant King
Or play Texas Tea and drill for some oil
You'll receive dividends for all of your toil

But those that dare play Dollars instead
One good win will increase their spread
Play the $2, $5, and $10 they say
Your pockets will fill with cash this way

The con deepens when a jackpot is won
The screams and yells from that lucky one
Everyone watches as they count out the bills
Thinking they too will soon share in the thrills

I remember the man who won $20,000 that day
"Welcome to gambling," I heard someone say
I knew the man would be back every week
For like a drug, that same "high" he would seek

Reminded me of the carnival that came to town
Sniffed out suckers like a shrewd bloodhound
It was chance and luck that came with a twist
Ruling and wriggling its conniving wrist

It's my turn, and 2000 "big ones" I took away
I was soon to be sucked in and led astray
Well, I gave it back and 2000 more in addition
Purposely planned was my impending perdition

Luckily I was saved by a mere payday loan
With interest rates that made strong men groan
No bills were paid and with this I went back
With another loss—derailed—off track

Casino, Casino, Casino Con
Here's the back of my head, I am forever gone
Some can handle your enticing advances
And can truly resist your "luck" and "chances"

But I came to a road that did diverge
And I allowed God's wisdom to finally emerge
For a fish out of water cannot survive
It must soon return to stay alive

God forgive my foolish ways
And direct and guide me the rest of my days
My resources I reserve for much better use
And I promise my time will not be loose

My health suffered from cigarette smoke
My habit left me completely broke
But I have unmasked the casino's cloak
And stand victoriously as God's mighty oak

Why Are You Marching?

Why are you marching?
Tell me, do you know?
I know why Dr. King went
But why do you go?

Young man, before you can march
You first have to stand
Stop wallowing in wages of welfare
Rise up, be a man

Young woman, know what you are fighting
And to what you are opposed
Stand up for what you believe
Keep your mind open and your legs closed

Dr. King said he'd been to the mountaintop
He said he looked over
Did he see the multitude of gangs?
Did he find anyone sober?

Was the Promised Land full of murder?
Did he see domestic violence and rape?
Did he see slaughtered unborn babies
Silenced, unable to escape?

Women marrying women
Men marrying men
Call it what you want
But God calls it sin

Why are you marching?
Tell me, do you know?
I know why Dr. King went
But why do you go?

If you honor Dr. King
Then also honor his beliefs
Remember his hopes and sorrows
Remember his joy and grief

Paul said follow me
As I follow the Savior
Always check your motives
And finely tune your behavior

Dr. King marched in Birmingham
He sat in jails; he sat in the street
He cried "We shall overcome!"
He never settled for defeat

Now segregation is no more
People of all colors stand with one mind
But why is it in the DES office
And the unemployment line?

We kicked God out of school
Now it's become like a jail
Blame the teacher, students, parents
But it is all of us who fail

What is your dream today?
And do you have the courage to act?
Or will you rest on the laurels of others?
Or just sigh and turn your back

Why are you marching?
Tell me, do you know?
I know why Dr. King went
But why do you go?

Barrack Obama is now president
Many think he's the first Black
Check your history more closely
Before him were five, as a matter of fact

Coolidge, Jefferson, Harding, Jackson, Lincoln
All with African blood of five percent
They decided passing instead of lynching
Was definitely more important

So, we have and had black leaders
They are symbols that we respect
But it is our turn to move forward
We need movers and shakers, and intellect

Why are you marching?
Tell me, do you know?
I know why Dr. King went
But why do you go?

Dr. King believed in God, the Bible,
And yes, even Jesus Messiah
His mighty faith moved a nation
But did they see what he saw?

Dr. King had a dream
And his dream came alive
He refused to give up
Until our people took that Freedom Ride

The doors finally flew open
Because Dr. King dared to knock
His courage came from within
From faith founded upon The Rock

Why are you marching?
Tell me, do you know?
I know why Dr. King went
But why do you go?

Young people find your voice
Shake the shackles of Alcohol, Porn, and Meth
Forsake the gangs; join God's family
Please choose life instead of death

Our ancestors fought long and hard
Suffered years so we could learn
Their bodies were brutally mutilated
And then their books brazenly burned

Through us their dreams came true
Our education is virtually free
We can earn a high school diploma
And then get a degree

You take it with you wherever you go
It's your lighthouse near and far
Just remember: true success in this life
Depends on you and Almighty God

So, young people, march on
Dr. King's torch lights your way
Keep marching, yes keep marching
Oh, there will be a better day!

Your Journey Notes & Reflections

Part Four

Reaching Back

Introduction

<u>This Hill I Climb</u> is the author's "poetic" 40-year journey on her road to Christ.

<u>Reaching Back</u> is the next stage of the author's life. The author has allowed us to travel to the final stage of her journey. We enjoyed and reveled in the glorious splendor of the heavenly realm. Now, lest our heavenly-mindedness cause us to forget to be earthly good, we now reach back. For through all of our teaching and preaching, we should be reaching.

We reach back and remember those who once shared the journey with us. We reach back and remember those whose time ended before reaching the mountaintop with us. However, their mountain experience was not ours. Their mountaintop was just another rung on our ascent. We mourned for a time and then through the grace and mercy of God, we committed them to His loving care. We know we'll see them again - this time in Jesus's perfection.

Lastly, we reach back and remember those who could no longer journey by our side. Their journey will continue, but with another companion. Their unions reflect God's purpose for his children. Their unions represent Messiah's wonderful return for his people. For we look forward to that day when our Savior will reach back and receive us unto himself, so that where He is we may be also. For when He reaches back with His angels, we know our journey in this life has reached its limit. We now begin another journey. Who but God really knows what kind it is? We care not. For as long as we're in the Father's tender and loving arms, it matters not *what* the journey is, it matters only that the journey *is*.

Twenty Years Young

My name is Washington Activity Center
Yes, I'm just barely twenty years old
For people that means your life's just starting
For me it's faded paint, cracks, and mold

But I, you see, am no ordinary building
There are special people within my walls
My history is rich and pure and precious
Mighty men have toured my halls

Yet, it started with the vision of a woman
A woman with God-anointed "helping hands"
She spoke of her goal to help the children
And others joined in to work her plans

After five years they were doing "Slimnastics"
People had fun dropping their pounds
But there was also a great pot luck lunch
And kids whirled frisbees around and around

There was karate and a Summer program
And of course the first Cultural Day
We had baton workshops and a sewing class
And the kids got to see the Giants play

By the time we celebrated my tenth anniversary
More people there to help clean and scrub
I remember Al Brooks was the mayor of Mesa
And there was Gene Lewis' Boxing Club

There were services for the senior community
Along with youth sports and special events
And finally the kids had a Head Start Program
Even I knew that made a whole lot of sense

After fifteen years we had some minor trouble
But they still taught the kids right from wrong
Help was on the way with Boyd on the Council
and even more so with Mayor Willie Wong

My building has seen some major renovations
I knew expansion was coming soon
Concessions and offices were moved around
And before long I had a new computer room

I was proud of my weight room and pool tables
And my new playground area was a kid's dream
But I later saw other projects and programs
Like the fantastic football and basketball team

There's been so much in just 20 short years
I've been around but I'm still pretty young
There's more in store for this Activity Center
Oh believe me, people, I've just begun.

In Memory of Tina

You all knew her as Tina
So meek, so quiet, so shy
But I will give her a new name
And a body that will never die

You may not understand my timing
For she lived twenty-six short years
But even a hundred can seem so few
If a man lives without hope and he fears

You may not understand all that I do
But know that always my will be done
For I take two lives and join them together
For the sole purpose of having a son

And he is one that I have anointed
For with power will he teach and preach
Though still a child he will yet minister
And a multitude of souls will he reach

My son know that with you I am pleased
In the love and devotion you gave
Let no one criticize the decisions you made
For by it, a soul you did save

You now know what my people must face
All will have an ultimate test
an you still love me, obey me, and trust me
Though I fulfill not your every request?

For healing have I put within your hands
Souls are touched as you play each chord
For spiritually the lame walk and the blind see
The dead are quickened when you wield my sword

Let your fingers dance on the music keys
Let your feet run and cut their step
Lift up your voice with the highest praise
And let your life be my living precept.

In Memory of Jerry

Yahweh (God) is nigh to those of a broken heart
For the loss of one you hold so dear
And we understand when you cry and moan
With hopes that out brother was still here
(Psalm 34:18)

But God will heal your broken heart
He'll even bind up your painful wound
You'll realize our brother's in a better place
Finally singing Redemption's tune
(Psalm 147:3)

Sometimes the righteous do perish
And taken away from the evil to come
And for the soldiers who sleep in Messiah
The mighty battle has been won
(Isaiah57:1)

Yahweh (God) saw his ways and led him
And will bring comfort to you who mourn
For we weep for one who sleeps
And we rejoice for one who's born
(Isaiah 57:18)

Yahweh (God) will give you beauty for ashes
And the oil of joy for mourning
The garment of praise for heaviness,
Because of our brother's eternal adorning
(Isaiah 61:3)

Yahweh (God) will turn your mourning into joy
His comfort will make you rejoice from sorrow
You'll remember that He's your ALL AND ALL
And HIS LOVING ARMS are there tomorrow
(Jeremiah 31:13b)

So do not sorrow as those without hope
For surely Jesus died and rose again
When He comes, He'll bring our brother
We'll meet again our brother and friend!
(1 Thessalonians 4:13-14)

Just remember his message on January tenth
He said, "Who's Plate Are You Eating From?"
Will you be filled with envy and anger
Or with agape love when Yahweh (God) does come?
(Romans 1:26-32)

And though you keep his love in your heart
He would rather you give it to those who remain
For by this you'll prove you're true sons of God
Maybe then we all can get on the Gospel train
(1 John 3)

In Memory of Andrew

I love you because you are a true brother in Messiah
I love you for the Holy Spirit which unites us in God's love
I love you for the kind and gentle husband you are to my sister
I love you because you give her such great joy
I love you because you bring out the best in her
I love you because you allow her to bring out the best in you
I love you for the teacher you are to me
I love you for the lessons and scriptures you have expounded for me
I love you for the power of God's words which roll off your tongue
I love you for the heavenly language you speak
I love you for the way you minister in song
I love you for the words of encouragement you give
I love you for the exhortation toward greatness you give
I love you for every prayer you offer, both spoken & unspoken
I love you for the laughter you bring to my soul
I love you because God does to.

When All Stood Still

To some he was impossible to understand
To God - the apostle in COGIC land
He ministered and recognized ministries
When others were too blind to see
I am so grateful he cleared away the trees
And denounced the fear within me
When I realized on whom the mantle fell
My first instinct was to cry and yell
But he was patient; he knew I would go higher
Though persecutions would ignite my ire
One day he said "My work here is done"
Oh, why was I that Chosen One?
For the path he tread was a lonely trail
Yet I knew with God I would not fail
I thanked him as his daughter
Put the phone to his ear
Him, in a coma, yet I knew he did hear
He arose long enough for God to get praise
Although I knew it was the end of his days
That Friday a train made the world stand still
I sat on the ground fighting away my chill
No reason to cry, yet tears could not hide
Bro. John had earned his gospel ride

The Purpose of Marriage

Some have wondered the Purpose of Marriage
And just why God ordained it so
Though there may be others – we know at least six
So please take notes, and do read slow

The first is developing true Companionship
Where oneness of spirit is the need
For God said you two will walk together
Once you both – are finally agreed
(Amos 3:3)

Second is Enjoyment where the bed is undefiled
And the particular principal is self-control
You both seek to meet the other's needs
Not "I want what I want" as the ultimate goal
(Hebrews 13:4)

Third is Completeness where both are made whole
For we know being single was never God's plan
Thus shouted Adam to his newly-formed Eve
"Now that's more like – Wo' - man!"
(Genesis 2:23)

Fourth is Fruitfulness from a blessed union
Where God said bring forth and multiply
And men being leaders such as you are
We know you'll be obedient and how hard you'll try
(Genesis 1:28)

Fifth, we know there must be Protection
"For my wife," men declare, "I'll lay my life down!"
Where's the proof you ask, and they'll state with a smile
"I ride in silence as my wife drives around town."
(Psalm 112)

Sixth, marriage must typify Messiah and His Bride
The divine union between Messiah and believers
Praise God for you both as you form His union
We know in all six you'll be over-achievers
(Ephesians 5:31-33)

Forever Hold Your Peace

The first marriages were by capture
The groom kidnaps the woman as best he can
He takes her away from her tribe
With the help of a warrior friend, the best man

The groom always places the bride on his left
To protect her at his side
With his right hand he wields his sword
To fight off others who would steal his bride

The couple makes sure no will find them
That is, not find them too soon
So the groom secures a hiding place
That's how we get the "honeymoon"

By the time the bride's family finds them
The bride is now ready to conceive
Her family now can only rejoice with them
And to her husband she is left to cleave

Now even though marriage by capture was common
Marriage by purchase was much preferred
To "wed" meant the groom made a vow of marriage
And paid money to the father, who had the last word

The groom's family told him who he was to marry
And the father of the bride gave the bride away
The groom never saw her until he lifted her veil
And whether or not she was appealing, brother got married that day!

Blue was the sign in biblical days of purity instead of white
The white wedding dress was not until
Year fourteen hundred and ninety nine
The bride and groom wore blue bands always at the hem
Something old, new, borrowed, but blue whatever they could find

It was customary for the bride
to toss her garter to the men
However due to male impatience
they would try to take the garter away
The groom was often not happy with this
So now the bride tosses the bridal bouquet

The rings joined the couples together
by hearts and destiny
The Romans believed the vein in the third finger
ran directly to the heart
So the wedding rings were made
of strong metal like iron
For it was considered not a good sign
if the rings fell apart

Originally, the wedding cake
was considered a symbol of fertility
Baked with wheat or barley
to be broken over the bride's head
Piled high in layers to challenge the couple
to kiss over the cake
No longer do we throw it at the couple
It makes more sense to eat it instead

So much for the world's traditions,
but what does it mean for us
Those who believe in Yahweh (God)
and always make Him our trust?

The groom is the first to enter the sanctuary
Initiating the covenant
with the one he will marry
Just as Messiah initiated for us
the covenant of salvation
His bride, Ysrayl will finally receive
her long-awaited coronation

The white wedding gown represents
purity of heart and of life
And the groom knows there's no other purer in heart
than the one soon to be his wife

The veil represents modesty and respect
And when lifted, signifies physical love can begin
Just as the veil of the temple was taken away
When Messiah fulfilled his promise to atone for all our sin

The white runner symbolizes a walk on holy ground
For the covenant is made before God and all witnesses around
The lamp stands are to be filled with oil
as we await our Father's return
Until such time as He takes us away,
forever in our hearts His word will burn

The two open their hands with mutual vows
Pledging their purpose, resources, and strength
Just as we look to God's outstretched hand
Whose resources exceed width, depth, breath, and length

The beginning of this marriage is signified
By proclaiming them husband and wife
Just as salvation begins with acceptance of Jesus
With baptism proclaiming a brand new life

And just as salvation is an ongoing process
And goes far beyond the joys of that day
So too, marriage, when the honeymoon is over
Faithfulness and commitment will keep emotions at bay

O' The Beat of Obedient Hearts

God gave His son, His most precious gift
The Son gave His life, Him, God would lift
And the Holy Ghost would come, and He too would give
Spiritual gifts so we could learn how to live

But if we speak with tongues of angels and men
and then in rebellion we continue to sin
Then we're merely making noise like a clang or a gong
For do we glorify Him when we continue in wrong?

We promise to bless Yahweh (God) at all times
And allow Him to renew our messed up minds
And in our mouths shall be His praise
For we want to please Him in all our ways

For love is patient, and kind, and good
And only through this, is marriage understood
To give *philos* or *eros* we never think twice
But agape love is born of spiritual sacrifice

With grace as the motive and unity as the goal
Jesus prayed that we all might be one whole
Randy and Pamala, by your commitment this day
You prove like Father like son in every way

As the sons of God your love is wide
And clearly without pretense, partiality, or pride
Consistently confirmed by the decision you've made
Confident in the way the foundation was laid

You see, God looked down and He watched his sprout
She was hesitant at first, not daring to come out
So many times they snatched up her roots
Polluted her soil and damaged her shoots

But finally she settled in sanctified ground
Knowing that here the true Word of God is found
And with all of her might she dug down deep
No longer a lamb, but a full grown sheep

The Spirit of God baptized her with fire
She cried "Yes, Father, I want to go higher!"
He purified her soul till she could take no more
And she shouted with joy from pulpit to the door

With a beautiful smile and a true willing heart
Two magnets God uses with skill and with art
She's ready to usher, to serve, and to teach
Wherever God places the souls in her reach

She's now a saved woman of flair
And of her spiritual credentials God is fully aware
To others my Sister, you need not prove a thing
Tell 'em "talk to Jesus," as they marvel at your ring

Now the two of you join hand in hand
To form the family that God had planned
An example of holiness wherever you go
A unity of love in which all can grow

Sweet Silent Symphony

Two souls sealed by the same Spirit of promise
Two magnificent minds renewed by the same Holy Ghost
Two rugged roads smoothed into one obedient path
Two ministries merged with one fervent focus
Two wills relinquished unto Messiah
Two holy heartbeats, delicately adapting
To the timing, tempo and subtleties of the other
Prayerfully producing the soft, spiritual,
symphony
That only the true followers of God can hear

Your Journey Reflection & Notes

Part Five

Redemption

Introduction

<u>This Hill I Climb</u> is the author's "poetic" 40-year journey on her road to Messiah.

<u>Redemption</u> is the next transition in the author's life. It has been at least 14 years after her 40-year journey. She finally understands and knows who she is, her true identify, her true roots, and her true heritage. She gives glory to Almighty God and patiently awaits her next assignment.

The author says she is ready to be redeemed from the curses that Yahweh (God) put upon her ancestors that extended until this age. The end of the Gentile rule has finally come. Like Dr. King, she has reached the mountaintop and looked over and has seen the "promised land." It flows with milk and honey. The curses have been lifted. Jesus Christ (Messiah Yahoshua) is soon to return for the remnant of the "apple of God's (Yahweh's) eye." She is determined to be in that number.

Halleluyah!

Redemption Time

Watch me, there I go
I can dance and I can shout
Finally give praise to God
I know what I'm shouting about

Father Yahweh (God) created man
From the dust of the earth
So now apart from Him
We know just what we're worth

Whoa now there we are
All around the globe
That's because everywhere
From slave ships we were sold

The good news is we're coming back
A remnant you will see
We have been redeemed
By our Savior on a tree

He rose again so we can have
The right to eternal life
But we must put aside our sins
Like jealousy and strife

Obey his laws and keep his word
And serve him from the heart
To these he said he'll never leave
And his Spirit won't depart

I know for a fact with all my heart
That Messiah's coming back
The moon will be as red as blood
And the sky it shall crack

The stars will fall from the sky
After we hear that sound
We'll be lifted up with those who sleep
When they are raised from the ground

Thank the Father in the highest
For the end of the Gentile rule
If you still don't know who you are
Then may you forever be a fool

What a happy day when I found out
That Messiah is dark like me
I belong to him and I always will
And this truth has set me free

Roots Dye but Never Die

Black roots may dye and fade away for a time
Like the gray in my hair for a song and a dime
But surely each and every cover up is known
Tricked as a child but wise when I'm grown

But these roots cannot die because of His blood
Created in His image with His hands and mud
Yet these physical houses only last so long
 Eternity with my Savior, that's where I belong

By No Other Name

Since the day I could walk with grandma's hands
I went to one of the churches throughout the lands
I heard them sing praises to Yahweh (God) who is God
They talked of a shepherd with a staff and a rod

When grandma was crying and I asked what was wrong
She said she was dying and to read the 23rd Psalm
She said child commit it to memory, each and every word
It was the best peace and comfort I'd ever heard

One day I gave my life to the one they called Messiah
Knowing my sins were forgiven brought a Halleluyah!
I studied to show myself approved without shame
Rejoicing now that I that I knew His real name

My roots and heritage stretched farther than I knew
Not hard to decipher what were lies and was true
A responsibility and call to go forth and to preach
No other name except Jesus, this I must teach

Holding Out and Moving Ahead

The road is hard, the journey is long
My feet are tired, my strength is gone
The enemy attacks whether I sleep or wake
But I've got to hold out for Yahweh (God)'s sake

With faith I go forward and will not turn back
God's Word will guide me and keep me on track
I want to see my Savior who died for me
Though weary and beaten as He hung on the tree

I can move up a little higher with joy in my heart
My Savior is still with me as He was from the start
The enemy can't hurt me, his plans are defeated
For at the right hand of God, my Savior is seated

Recognizing the Counterfeit

Counterfeit or real
For myself I must make this choice
Then and only then
Can my soul in peace rejoice

By their fruits you will know them
By what hangs on their tree
Are the Fruit of the Spirit manifest
Or the works of the flesh do you see?

Taking the Good with the Bad

First the bad news
Then the good news
One for my appealing
The other for my healing

I must change the way I think
With reason, not instinct
Let His word be my light
Not my strength or my might

A positive outlook on life
Amid many trials and strife
Whatever is true, honest, and pure
No matter what I have to endure

Whatever is lovely and of good report
Thoughts like these I won't abort
If there be any virtue; if there be any praise
On this may I ponder for the rest of my days

Not Without My Armor

Out of the devil's mouth proceeds only lies
Built with slandering stones and sticks
We need only to put on the whole armor
To withstand his tyranny of tricks

One demonic dart after another
He never learns for he's uncouth
His deception has no lasting power
Against our God-given belt of truth

The enemy conjures up evil spirits
Beings of wrath and beings of wraith
Let them come; let them enter
No match for righteousness, salvation, and faith

When all is said and all is done
And the enemy has ranted and roared
We can now end his devilish discussion
With Yahweh (God)'s trusted two-edged sword

The Right to Choose Life

Yahweh (God) shall supply all my needs
According to his mercy and grace
No more will I defile His temple
To bring reproach and to bring disgrace

The birth of a child is so precious
And rebirth in Messiah brings light
A child and a ministry can both surely perish
While we argue about what's wrong or what's right

Finishing the Race

I must move ahead and persevere
Despite the discouragement of what I hear
The enemy wants me to give up and turn back
And to keep my focus on what I still lack

I know Yah (God) shall supply all my need
The same as in the beginning when I first believed
The journey is hard and the road is long
But I still marvel at what he's brought me from

The tears are many and so are the pains
How can I withstand the winds and rains
How long Father before you call me home
This is not my place, not where I belong

I know you are with me, come what may
I cannot turn back, nor your trust betray
So, I move forward in your strength and power
Awaiting complete redemption in that fateful hour

Taking Out the Garbage

The words of my mouth
At times are my snare
What are my true motives
When I show that I care

My words must be pure
My conversation without spite
God knows every intent
Whether for wrong or for right

My Turn Is Coming

I will not envy others
Nor be jealous of their gift
I will not be as the chaff
Nor the wheat that you sift

Praise you Messiah
For the blessings that you give
I know you will provide for me
Every day that I live

I Feel Therefore I Am

Suffering and pain I seem to endure
But no doctor on earth has my cure
Yahweh (God) has given me all that I need
Herbs of the field and life in the seed

His hand is upon me and I feel his touch
Oh why, I cry, does he love me so much
He gave me all that I need for healing
So it is only to him I will be appealing

Fit As a Fiddle

Enter into his courts with thanksgiving
Enter into his courts with praise
My instrument must be healthy
And finely tuned when it plays

This instrument is my body
The holy temple where Yahweh (God) dwells
I must not defile this holy place
With the drug of men that fails

A Position of Dignity

Something I've heard
That's rather absurd
Work is a foul four-letter word

A job they won't start
Because they haven't the heart
Tragically their money and they do part

Yet God is the one
Who said through his Son
On the cross my work here is done

Our work is to do
Like the diligent few
Who worked as the witnesses grew

No more idle hands
Of the ant we are fans
As we faithfully fulfill God's plans

Death Be Not Proud

I stood at my crossroad
While he rode a cross to the tree

I contemplated what I would be giving up
While he gave up his life for me

I know nothing could be compared
To the agony Messiah shared

But He is the greatest like Muhammad Ali
Who floats like a butterfly and stings like a bee

Stripping sin and death of their eternal sting
Those two dare not show their faces in Messiah's ring!

Your Journey Notes & Reflections

About The Author

Dr. Elizabeth A. James (E.A. James) has been writing for over 40 years. She is a licensed and ordained minister and has been President and Founder of Fast And Indispensable Temporary Help (F.A.I.T.H.) Ministries, Inc. since February, 1999. She is also the Editor-in-Chief of FM Publishing Company (2009) and Senior Managing Director of Geri Lorraine Enterprises, LLC (2000). In 2014, she became a supplier, independent marketer, and supporter with TAG Team Marketing International and a dedicated member of the Black Business Network.

After attending over 10 colleges, she has a doctorate in Theology & Biblical Counseling, a master's in Education, bachelor's degree in English, and major course work in subjects such as Business Management, Biomedical Engineering, Pre-Med, and Chemistry.

In addition to many other accomplishments, E.A. James has received the Woman of Excellence Award, is a member of blackwritersconnect.com, and has won several awards for her poetry. She is currently a business consultant, certified teacher, and a Nationally-Certified Manager of Program Improvement.

Titles by E.A. James:

Spiritual Cosmetics for the Soul (devotionals)
The Last Visitor (historical fiction)
Being a Well Body of Believers (nonfiction)
This Hill I Climb (poetry)
The Reason Why I Sing (poetry/songs)
Driving Tips for BOOHs (Bats Out of Hell) (satire)
7-Day Emergency Help for OWIACs (Of Whom I Am Chief) (devotionals)
Why I Should Hate Men, But Don't (nonfiction)
Will Work for Food, Family & Freedom (nonfiction)
Casino Con: An Eye-Opening Look From the Inside Out (nonfiction)

Publication and Catalog Ordering Information

To get other books by E.A. James in print, e-book, kindle, or to inquire about screenplay production rights:

FM Publishing Company
P.O. Box 215
Cherokee, NC 28719

Website: fmpublishingcompany.com

Email: fmpublishing@cox.net

Fax: 800-518-1219

www.ingramcontent.com/pod-product-compliance
Lightning Source LLC
Chambersburg PA
CBHW070450050426
42451CB00015B/3417